D0332784

Books are to be returned on or before, the last date shown below.

29 APR 2013

19 DEC 2013

2 2 MAR 2013

Jam
He tr
cour
ofter
is a p

E
beer
watc
writin

Raise
Garb
his m
miles
surfac

rs.
of
le
ch

as
st
of

s
h
o
s

Also available from Macmillan

The Works 6
Every kind of poem you will ever need for assembly
Chosen by Pie Corbett

Why Otters Don't Wear Socks
Poems by Roger Stevens

Behind the Staffroom Door
Poems by Brian Moses

TIME TRAVELLING UNDERPANTS

POEMS BY JAMES CARTER

Illustrated by Chris Garbutt

Macmillan Children's Books

First published 2007 by Macmillan Children's Books
a division of Macmillan Publishers Limited
20 New Wharf Road, London N1 9RR
Basingstoke and Oxford
www.panmacmillan.com

Associated companies throughout the world

ISBN: 978-0-330-44709-6

Text copyright © James Carter 2007
Illustrations copyright © Chris Garbutt 2007

The right of James Carter and Chris Garbutt to be identified
as the author and illustrator of this work has been asserted by them
in accordance with the Copyright, Designs and Patents Act 1988.

All rights reserved. No part of this publication may be
reproduced, stored in or introduced into a retrieval system, or
transmitted, in any form or by any means (electronic, mechanical,
photocopying, recording or otherwise), without the prior written
permission of the publisher. Any person who does any unauthorized
act in relation to this publication may be liable to criminal
prosecution and civil claims for damages.

1 3 5 7 9 8 6 4 2

A CIP catalogue record for this book is available from
the British Library.

Typeset by Tony Fleetwood
Printed and bound in Great Britain by Mackays of Chatham plc, Kent

This book is sold subject to the condition that it shall not,
by way of trade or otherwise, be lent, resold, hired out,
or otherwise circulated without the publisher's prior consent
in any form of binding or cover other than that in which
it is published and without a similar condition including this
condition being imposed on the subsequent purchaser.

*For my top two intrepid travellers, Lauren and Madeleine,
with all my love. Happy travels.*

With one poem for Sarah, and a special thanks to Ian.

Contents

0th Birthday Poem

I
was
born
on my
birthday
in my
birthday
suit
I
was
pinky
and
wrinkly
and
ever so
cute –
and
ever so
bald
or so
I've
been
told
cos
I
don't
recall
being
0
years
old

Amazing Inventions

When I was 10
I really believed
that in the future
there'd be
such *AMAZING INVENTIONS* as
FLYING CARS
UNDERWATER CARS
MACHINESthatcouldmakeanyflavour*crisp*youaskedfor

day trips to the moon
video phones
                    and robot dogs & cats
in e v e r y home
and
M O S T   I M P O R T A N T L Y
bubble gum

that could make you

INVISIBLE

So you can imagine
just how d i s a p p o i n t e d I was
when I got to 20
and none of them
had come true

So you can also imagine
how e x t r e m e l y m i f f e d I was
when I got to 40
and still none of them
had come true

Until they do
I'd like to say
do you know what
I reckon
is THE MOST **AMAZING INVENTIONS**
us humans
have come up with so far?

Have a think

Our brains
come up with them

Our mouths
get rid of them

This poem
is made of them

Words

Go tell the world
  that words aren't cheap
for like the trees
  their roots go deep
for like the winds
  they blow your way
for like the seeds
  they won't all stay
for like the clouds
  they have such grace
for like the seas
  they roar and rage
for like the sun
  they feed you light
for like the moon
  they dwell at night
for like the sky
  they're made of air
go tell the world
  treat words with care

What Will I Be When I Grow Up?

Mum says: '**HAPPY**.'

Dad says: '**Older – and taller**.'

My sister Kate says: 'Just as . . . nice!'

My mate Sam says: '**Still my best friend**.'

Aunty Jessie says: '*Anything you want to be*.'

Uncle Jack says: '**An adult!**'

My teacher says: '**WISER**.'

And Gran says: '*Brilliant*.'

And I say: How do they know?

Time-Travelling Underpants

A few words of W A R N I N G to those that own them

1. DON'T SHOW YOUR UNDERPANTS TO ANYONE.
You don't go around showing people your other pants do you? Do you?!?

2. DON'T TELL ANYONE ABOUT YOUR UNDERPANTS.
If you do, watch out! They might try and take them off you when you're not looking.

3. WASH YOUR UNDERPANTS.
Do you really need to know why?

4. REMEMBER: UNDERPANTS ARE UNDERPANTS.
NOT places to store pocket money or unwanted sprouts.

5. DON'T SLEEP IN YOUR UNDERPANTS.
You might just knock the time switch by accident and wake up in a cave next to a hungry sabre-toothed tiger.

6. DON'T LEND YOUR UNDERPANTS TO ANYONE.
Especially the school dinner ladies.

7. DON'T FORGET TO HOLD ON TO THE SIDES OF YOUR PANTS
and to chant OUT LOUD the Time-Travelling Underpants Owners' Mantra before each time-trip:

My pants are warm and free from grime
and as I journey far in time
I travel safe with peace
of mind: my pants
are clean –
so I'll be
fine!

Off the Wall

Our teacher told us
that some 30,000 years ago
early humans
painted pictures
of their world
on the walls
of their caves –
pictures
that still
enchant us
today

By the light
of a crackling fire
they daubed their images –
scenes of people
and animals
living their lives –
now reminders
to us
of how
we used to be

30 minutes ago
my sister Emily
drew a family picture
of my mum
my dad
and me
and our cat Albert
on the kitchen wall
and I thought
it was pretty good

It was only up there
a matter of seconds
before my mum
wiped it off
with a cloth

Mums
must have been different
back then

Time Capsule

On past the cabbages
round the side of the shed
way way down
in the thick loamy soil
lies my time capsule

It's waiting
for the people
of the future
to make sense
of what my teacher calls
'our mementos
from the 21st century'

But what if
the shoebox
gets all soggy?

And what if
slugs and worms and weevils
come and
nibble nibble nibble
it all away?

And what if
nobody ever
finds it
anyway?

And what if
I don't actually
tell my teacher
about digging it all up
and rescuing
my favourite blue marble
my first wobbly tooth
and Woof, my lovely old pyjama-case dog

Not that I need these
any more or anything
because I don't
actually
it's true
really

And anyway
I could
put them up
in the attic
instead

Where they'd
be much easier
to find

So there

Night Soup (a simple recipe)

Take . . .

A slither of moon
a nip in the air
a sprinkle of stars
a creak from a stair

Add plenty of dark
the slink of a cat
(with cold green eyes)
a loop from a bat

The patter of rain
the whine of a dog
the taste of a dream
the wisp of a fog

The whoosh of a train
a sniff or a snore
the swoop of an owl
then stop – no more

Then stir it around
and bring to the boil
season with cinammon
add olive oil

Now let it go cold
and serve quite late
and all
        that is left
                to do
                    is wait . . .

Talking Time

Not only the day but also the night
I am the coming and going of light

The growing and turning of shadows on land
the falling of sand, that watch on your hand

The arc of the moon, the tug of the tides
the till of the fields, the sun as it hides

The here and the now and the way back when
In hide & seek games: the counting to ten

Your birthday, your diary, the lines on your face
the start and the finish of every race

Measure me, treasure me, do as you will
I'll drag or I'll fly but I'll never stay still

If I am your rhythm, then you are my rhyme
we live for each other, and my name is time

A
very tiny
but very
loud poem
in
which
the narrator of
the poem – wearing only his
pyjamas and slippers – goes out
into his back garden one very dark
and very stormy night to search –
without a torch – for his very scruffy
but very cute tabby cat Mr Wibble –
yet instead of finding Mr Wibble
he picks up a very timid but
very pointy little ball that is
in fact a hedgehog:

YIKES
SPIKES

Wobbly Bin Bag

Quite late one night
having called the cat in
I'm closing the back door
thinking it's darker and quieter
than the darkest and quietest night
anywhere ever
when I hear
a rustling sound
coming from around the corner.

I switch on the outside light
and find that the rustling
is coming from
the bin bag full of rubbish
and the rustling is getting
louder and louder
and the bag is now wobbling
from side to side
so I rush back indoors.

Silly thing! I say to myself.
       It can't hurt me.
            It's only a field mouse
                 or a vole
                     or a rat. A RAT????!!!!!!

Please not a rat, I think.
       It might jump on me.
            Rat's don't jump up on you, do they?
            Do they?!?

Perhaps I should help it, I think.
  It might be in trouble, I think.
    If it can crawl *in* the bag, it can crawl *out* again, I think.

The next morning
still in my pyjamas
I'm back out there
and I see a hole in the bag
and a little note
written in scribbly rodenty writing:

You know those five mouldy blueberries?
They were absolutely lovely.
Any more would be much appreciated.
    Best wishes,
        A. Rat (Mrs)

Which is a bit weird really
because I'm sure
they were raspberries.

White Horse

Horse on hill
Horse so still
Horse can't walk
Horse all chalk

Starry night
Moon so bright
Horse in sky
Horse can fly

No one know
No one see
Horse can roam
Horse so free

Fly by night
Stand by day
White horse dream
Her life away

Reindeer Haikus

Reindeer skeleton
stood in a dark museum
remembering snow

remembering lights
flashing flickering pink green
then a shot goes out

and the sky goes black
and the silence hangs heavy
as snow turns to red

Icy Morning Haikus

On a frozen pond
a small dog is nervously
attempting to skate

Way up in the tree
a black cat grins with delight
watching and waiting

Beneath the clear ice
a big fish wonders if all
dogs walk on water

Moving House

ANTS!

Bit by bit
and day by day
those critters took my house away

Monday morning: 8 o'clock
to start the week – a nasty shock
my breakfast wasn't there at all
I found it walking down the wall

Flake by flake, my favourite crunch
was soon to be an insects' lunch
they took the sugar, spoon and bowl
and the packet – ate it whole

Bit by bit . . .

They drank my tea, removed my chair
whatever next – my underwear?
well, that was later, as you'll see
their first concerns were culinary

Next the cupboards – cat food too
they sucked the water out the loo
they took the fridge right through the door
(a thousand ants can gnaw and gnaw)

Bit by bit . . .

Wednesday morning, I went spare
the house and me: completely bare
no clothes or cupboards, walls or doors
windows, stairs or even floors

Bit by bit . . .

By Thursday morning, 8.02
the roof was off, the front was too
By Friday night there's no more home
(and yet they've left the garden gnome)

Bit by bit . . .

I look around, the garden's gone
no grass or shrubs or shed or pond
so – please could someone give a home
to naked me . . . plus garden gnome?

Mary Didn't Have a Little Lamb

No.

Mary had a little slug
its skin was tough and green
and when the slug refused to budge
oh gosh, was there a scene!

You should have heard our Mary yell
'I need you slug – for Show & Tell!
It's time for school – now come on, please!'
she even got down on her knees

But slug was not one to be swayed
and poor old Mary was dismayed
when slug set off and walked to school
all four miles – the crazy fool!

So how to end this oddly tale?
did slug succeed, give up or fail?
well, slug did make it to the gate
(of the school) some two years late

One half-term – so had to wait
till Monday morning – by the gate
but having come so very far
was flattened by a teacher's car

Monday Morning 10 a.m.

At times like these
he dreams of being
somewhere else
altogether

More often
than not
he's out
in space
freefloating
over the earth –
watching
the clouds
twist and twirl
over the great
blue oceans

Anything
to get out
of that spelling test

School Today

Mum said: 'What did you learn
          at school today?'

And you said: 'I'm not sure.
          I went to the loo
          and I think I missed it.'

Pop to the . . .

Better than a garden shed – the
perfect place to rest your head:
it's where you go to be alone – the
room that has the royal throne.
By other names it's also known:
the bog, the loo, the lavatory
the little room, the WC.

!!!!

!!!!

!!!!

!!!!

!!!!

!!!!

!!!!

Why not go and take a look?
Chill in there, or read a
book. Take your
time, remember
though –
somebody
might need to go!

The Little Boy Said

'Can I play too?'
the little boy said
'I'll be a tree
and I'll stand at the back'

The big kids kept on talking

'Can I play too?'
the little boy said
'I'll be a cat
and I'll keep real quiet'

The big kids kept on talking

'CAN I PLAY TOO?'
the little boy said
'I'LL BE A BALLOON
AND I'LL KEEP OUT THE WAY.'

The big kids kept on talking

Nobody heard
the little boy cry
                'wheeeeee!!! . . .'
                                    as he rose up
                                        into the sky

The big kids kept on talking

Numbers

As numbers go
44
is a good one:

It's two little birds
standing one-legged
in a two-bird queue

But
22
being a couple of swans
(perhaps gliding across
a moonlit lake
studded with a thousand
celestial stars)
is even better
                and a bit more posh

Empty Bucket

It was late afternoon
and I'd been peering
into the rockpools
for absolutely ages
when this boy comes over
points at his bucket
and says '14 shrimps
        5 crabs
        2 dogfish.'

'Wow!' I say.

'What've you got?' he says.

'Nothing' I say.

'Nothing?' he says. 'Nothing?'

'No' I say.

Then his little brother
comes over
points at his bucket
and says '3 crabs
          4 shrimps.'

'Fantastic!' I say.

'What've you got?' he says.

'Nothing' I say.

'Nothing?' he says. 'Nothing at all?'

'No' I say.

Then their little sister
comes over
points at her bucket
and says '1 starfish.'

'Brilliant!' I say.

She looks into my bucket
and says 'What's in there then?'

'Nothing' I say.

'Nothing?' she says. 'Nothing at all? How old are you?'

'44' I say

The Big Things

Early evening
I'm sitting in my favourite tree
gazing at the moon
in the pale summer sky
just thinking

Thinking about the big things:
like time
and infinity
and the cosmos
and how our little misty marble
of a planet
keeps spinning around
in that great murky soup
we call space

When Keith –
my next door neighbour –
peers over the fence
and says 'What you doin'
up there then?'

And I say
'Well, Keith – I was thinking
about the unstoppableness of time
and the smallness of me
and the wopping great bigness of space
and things.'

And Keith says 'Oh, right.'

And I jump down
from the tree
climb over the fence
and say 'Keith?
Do you ever think about time
and space and life
and what it all means and stuff?'

And Keith says 'Fancy a game of footie?'

And I say 'Do you, Keith?
And do you think about
how the planets all turn together
like the cogs of a massive cosmic clock?'

And Keith says 'Look, you playing
footie or what?'

And I say 'No seriously, Keith,
do you think about it?'

And Keith says 'I'll go in goal.'

And I say 'Oh . . . whatever.'

Fantasy Christmas List

The thing
about going round
to Robert Baker's house
is that something
that little bit different
would happen
every time

For instance
one Saturday afternoon
in June
we were up in Robert's bedroom
and I said 'What shall we do, then?'
and Robert said 'A fantasy Christmas list, of course.'
and I said 'Er . . . OK . . . why not?'

When we'd finished
Robert showed me
his list of things:

    A bright red electric guitar
    A very fast sports car
    A trip to Australia
    A house in America with a swimming pool
    A magic carpet
    A naked lady
    A real magic wand

And then I showed Robert my list of things:

A giant conker
A massive box of cheese-and-onion crisps
A new trainspotting annual
A huge bottle of cream soda
A naked lady

Then Robert
got in a right old huff
said 'You copied
my naked lady,
didn't you?'
and made me
cross it off my list

I didn't really want one anyway

SANTA:
Ace Guy or Strange Bloke?

Shows up every Christmas without fail.

Always knows what you've asked for.

Never forgets where you live (even if you've moved)

Takes nothing in return:

Ace guy.

Strange bloke:

Answers everything with a 'Ho, ho, ho!'

Nowhere to be seen from January to November.

Thought to live at the North Pole with *elves* and *reindeer*.

And who else would put on a red costume – rush around like a mad thing – visit every single house in the whole world – dump off thousands of presents for people he doesn't even know – AND eat *several million mince pies?*

The Village

The village still
beneath the hill
dressed in white
wrapped in night

A pigeon flaps
its paper wings
church bells chime
the village sings

Home from Mass
up the stairs
the village sleeps
quite unaware

A stranger comes
but not by road
to pass around
his heavy load

More snow falls
day is dawning
the village wakes:
Christmas morning

Call Me (Kenning #1)

Toe warmer
    toast maker
forest eater
    water hater
dragon lover
    light giver
candle melter
    plague ridder
London killer
    coal bringer
heavy smoker
    people choker

Yes I'm cruel
    but I'm no liar
I'm the one
    that you call . . . fire

What on Earth? (Kenning #2)

Shapeshifter
  ship lifter
beach crasher
  cliff basher
sin washer
  loo flusher
world-wider
  firefighter
life taker
  life saver
make-a-cuppa
  washer-upper
store-in-tower
  hydro-power
April shower
  feed-a-flower

I can be ice
    or steam or snow
        but just for now
            I'm . . . H$_2$O

A tree
is not like you and
me – it waits around quite
patiently – catching kites and
dropping leaves – reaching out to touch
the breeze . . . A tree all day will stand and stare
clothed in summer, winter: bare – it has no shame
or modesty . . . Perhaps its generosity is the greatest in
the world – it gives a home to every bird, every squirrel,
feeds them too – to every dog it is a loo . . . And after dark
what does it do? Catch a falling star or two? Shimmy
in the old moonlight? Or maybe have a conker fight?
A tree can give an awful lot: the wood to make a
baby's cot – pencils, paper, tables, chairs – lolly
sticks as well as stairs . . . Without a tree we
could not live – a tree, it seems just
loves to give –
but us:
we
chop
we
take
we
burn –
that's
what we
do in return

Big Mother

You don't get much more wild than me
and yet my child, we're family
but what I really ought to do
is introduce myself to you

I'm a gardener, that's my role
weeds to woods, I grow them all
celebrating every season
that's my life, my way, my reason

Listen now – beneath the ground:
hear that gentle rumbling sound?
there, that's me: I'm waiting, humming
my big summer gig is coming!

Love the damp, the dark, the night
love the wind, the heat, the light
but need the rain and need the sun –
help me grow up big and strong

Cut me down and I'll be back
crawling out through every crack
first a little dandelion
next a forest – I ain't lyin':

When I say I can't be tamed
I'm always there, but rarely named
I'll always win – and that I'll wager
I'm your other Mother – Nature

Road

Put your ear
against this road
and you will hear
the wheels that rolled

The souls that passed
the stories told
of journeys made
from young to old

The towns that rose
the dreams that fell
the weary resting
by the well

The hopeful going
back for more
the soldier coming
home from war

The horses' hooves
the driving rain
the travellers' tales
the circus train

The songs the cries
the laughs the lies
the lovers lost in
long goodbyes

And though this road
will let you roam
it's always there
to take you home

Happy Poem

Happy as a rainbow
happy as a bee
happy as a dolphin
splashing in the sea

Happy as bare feet
running on the beach
happy as a sunflower
happy as a peach

Happy as a poppy
happy as a spoon
dripping with honey
happy as June

Happy as a banjo
plucking on a tune
happy as a Sunday
lazy afternoon

Happy as a memory
shared by two
happy as me . . .
when I'm with you!

Your Picture

You draw a picture
of me. You do a big round blob
with googly eyes, huge hands
and sticky-up hair. Underneath
you write my name
with the J back to front.
I hide the picture.
You want it back.
I say I want to keep it
forever. Please do me
another, I say. No, you say.
It's your best ever
picture, I say. You agree.

That night I sneak
into your room, steal
your picture and whisper
that I promise to take
good care of it.

And I will.

Write Your Name

Write your name
with a stick
in the sand

Write your name
in the snow
with your hand

Write your name
on a board
with a chalk

Write your name
in the air
as you talk

Write your name
as you breathe
on glass

Write your name
with your friends
in class

Write your name
all curly
and small

Write your name
all pointy
and tall

Write your name
in the dark
at night

Write your name
in the sky
with a kite

Write your name
whatever you do –
write your name
to celebrate
YOU!

Inside

Now
you
may think
I'm walking tall
I'm talking big
I've got it all –
but here inside
I'm ever so shy
I sometimes cry
I'm curled in a ball
I'm no feet small

no	I'm
not	big
not	tall
at	all

Be You

This poem simply wants to say
take good care upon your way
beware, the path may not be clear
and when your goal may not be near

Don't let others make you stray
guide yourself and feel your way
find out what you want to do
and where it feels just right for you

When you're off, so far from home
often you might feel alone
don't hide inside or be ashamed
everybody feels afraid

Do not worry if you find
you may want to change your mind
yet whatever you may do
just be true and just be you

Found It Yet?

You'll find it
>>> in a four-leaf clover
>>> or
>>> in the heart of your beloved
>>> or
>>> on the end of your glove
>>> or
>>> all over

You'll find it
>>> if you really look for it

Love You More

Do I love you
to the moon and back?
No I love you
more than that

I love you to the desert sands
the mountains, stars
the planets and

I love you to the deepest sea
and deeper still
through history

Before beyond I love you then
I love you now
I'll love you when

The sun's gone out
the moon's gone home
and all the stars are fully grown

When I no longer say these words
I'll give them to the wind, the birds
so that they will still be heard

I love you

World of Weird

In the world of Weird
all the girls wear beards
and the boys keep bees in their beds
the girls dig holes and live like moles
and the boys grow trees on their heads

In the world of Weird
all the oranges are blue
and the lemons are as sweet as can be
bananas are round and grow in the ground
or down at the bottom of the sea

In the world of Weird
all the fish can fly
and the chips are fried in lakes
the dogs love cats: with sauce, of course –
served up on silver plates

Now how do you get
to the world of Weird? –
where is it? where is it? where?
hop on a bee – pop over the sea
then give us a call when you're there!

Sorry Sorry Sorry

Sorry, I wasn't listening
to a single word you said
I drifted off into the mist
that grew inside my head

Sorry, I wasn't listening
I didn't hear a sound:
I went where dreams of dreams have dreams
and sky and ground swap round

Sorry, I wasn't listening
aliens were at the door
asking for directions to
the planet XR4

Sorry, I wasn't listening
some pirates came for me
first I had to walk the plank
and then I made them tea

Sorry, I wasn't listening
I don't know what went on
could you say it one more time –
hang on – where've you gone?

Boris
the boredest boy in the world

Before he reached the age of one
Boris knew life wasn't fun
for this is what his mother heard –
Boz's first and favourite word:

'BORED!'

'What's that, Bo-bo? Mumsie cried
Boris looked at her and sighed
too bored to say the word once more
he toddled out and closed the door

'BORED!' And so began his life
of tedium and humdrum strife
bored of being bored and not
Boz was bored no matter what

Boris Horis Wallace Norris
(son of Doris and of Maurice)
had the most exciting folks
full of life and love and jokes

These two could not have been more fun
and tried their darnedest for their son –
but little tricks and magic stuff
and jolly japes were not enough

'BORED!' he cried for years to come
even though his dad and mum
enticed their one and only child
with entertainments weird and wild

Whilst other kids had friends to play
the Ns had circus troupes to stay
Bozzer always sat and snored

'BORED! BORED! BORED! **BORED!**'

When Mr N would swallow fire
and Mrs N walked tightrope wire
and clowns would set the place alight
Boris had an early night

Seals-a-singin', dogs-a-disco
failed to thrill their little kid so
Ma and Pa went on a tour
to chivvy up their grizzly bore

Paris, New York, Moscow, Rome
everywhere became their home
what they didn't see and do!
all to no avail, mind you

The pyramids did not impress
what did Bozzer say? You guess!
Other places did not please:
Mount Everest, the Seven Seas

Same with skiing in Peru
treasure hunts in Katmandu
bungee jumping in Jamaica
deep-sea diving off Australia

On they went and all the while
Bozzer never raised a smile
not one 'Thank you. That was great!'
so his poor folks grew irate

Back home, the Ns just watched TV
they slobbed and slouched in misery
'What's up with you?' young Boris roared
Shh! they said and whispered:

Learn
how to play
AIR GUITAR
in only 20 seconds
or your money back !!!

Just follow these 7 Simple Steps to Air Guitar Heaven:

1. MAKE SURE YOUR AIR GUITAR IS IN TUNE: pretend to fiddle with the tuning pegs and make some weird tuning sounds with your mouth.

2. DON'T JUST STRUM IT MADLY: make it look like you know what you're doing. Play a mean and moody rock riff. And why not take a solo? And don't forget to use the old whammy bar.

3. IF YOU HAVEN'T GOT EXTREMELY LONG HAIR, FAKE IT BABY!: pretend you've got hair that hangs all the way down your back. Now swish it from side to side and backwards and forwards as you're playing. Yeahhhhhh!

4. GET SOME COOL POSES GOING ON: try the 'windmill' strum or the leg-in-the-air 'duck walk'. Get down on your knees and sway wildly from side to side. If in doubt, just make stuff up!

5. PULL SOME REALLY WEIRD FACES: practise in the mirror first, you don't want to look too weird. You could try closing your eyes and a) pretending your teeth are glued together, or b) better still, pretending your tongue is glued to your chin. Cooooool!

6. CHECK NO ONE IS LOOKING: then check again. And again.

7. TURN THE STEREO UP AND GET . . .
ROCKIN'!!!

Now when you play your air guitar – don't think you're a superstar: you're a rockin' megastar – you are! you are! you are! you are! you are! you are! you are!

The Spider

A gentle reminder
dear reader
the spider
h a t e s humans
     it's true
would I lie to you?

Why do you think
it waits in the sink
the bath or the loo –
To say a 'Hello!'
or a 'How do you do?'

Oh no, dear reader
the opposite's true:
it hangs about there
all ready to scare
          the pants
              off of
                you

Clever Turtle, Hungry Shark

A shark was cruising for a bite
when suddenly there came in sight
a turtle – fat and fit to eat
'Mmm . . .' said Shark, 'I spy some meat!'

'Wait a mo!' the turtle cried
'Think about this. Have you tried
some turtle soup or turtle stew
or turtle-on-the-barbeque?'

'I don't much care for talking food
or turtles full of attitude!'
Sharkie snapped. Then opened wide –
poor Turtle had nowhere to hide

So looked big toothie in the face:
'Maybe we could have a race?'
'A race? What for? the big fish said
'I'd rather eat you up instead!'

'Well . . .' said Turtle, 'think of it –
a race would prove you're very fit –
the fastest creature of the seas.'
'Ah!' grinned Shark, so smugly pleased

Soon appeared a massive crowd
cheering, jeering, whooping loud
seagulls, starfish, crabs and cod
the race began – but oh, how odd

Turtle swiftly swam and swam
but Sharkie had a different plan:
first he thought he'd grab some lunch
just a crab or two to munch

Sharks are sharks and never know
when their tums are full and so
When Sharkie stopped off for a bite –
boy, he had an appetite!

This is what old Toothie scoffed:
seagulls, say some twenty odd
loads of lobsters, in their shells
several thousand squid as well

It's hard to pity such a beast
whose greed should lead to such a feast
but clever Turtle won that race
for Sharkie sank without a trace

This tale may seem pure pointlessness
but no, it's not – the moral's this:
if you want to win a race
first of all don't stuff your face

The
What to Do
When You Meet
a Puffin Eating Fish
Poem

say
nuffin
to a puffin
if its beak is
full of fish – do
not interrupt this
bird with its bestest
dish – to talk is rude
when chewing food
– so wait a while
and maybe
smile –
and
let that
puffin finish off its
scaly slippy fishy scoff

The What to Do If You Find a Sleeping Tiger Poem

I know it is extremely rare
to find a sleeping tiger there –
by your bed or on the stair
but don't be scared: be prepared!

A tiger leads a busy life
full of hunting, stress and strife
so leaves the jungle to recover
has a nap some place or other

If you chance upon this beast
do try not to be its feast
a word of caution: please beware
approach this cat with utmost care

Don't gape or gawp at what you've found
don't you make the slightest sound
breathe not or you will feel the breath
of tiger wrath – then instant death

See those paddy paws and claws?
gnashing teeth and awesome jaws?
they're what make the tiger king
of everyone and everything

And eyes of amber, shut so tight?
golden coat with stripes of night?
tail that twitches, swats the air? –
perhaps it senses that you're there . . .

To wake the tiger is unwise
unless you also have nine lives
admire the beast, then when you're done
the best thing you can do is . . . run!!!

Tiger's Dream

It's always the same:
the bars of the cage vanish
then she slinks away

Who Knows About UFOs?

If **UFO**s are **U**nidentified **F**lying **O**bjects -
whose job is it to identify them?

And, once identified, does a **UFO** become an **IFO**?

And, if a **UFO** can no longer fly –
perhaps due to a technical problem –
does it become a **UO**?

And, if I threw my slipper in the air –
and nobody knew what it was –
would it too be a **UFO**?

I think I'll file these questions under
Utterly **F**antastic **O**bservations

The Amazing Adventures of SPACE BOY
featuring
COSMIC CAT

Every space mission
takes an age of preparation

Every Saturday
on returning from the Mega Store

Watched and guided
by the silent Cosmic Cat
Space Boy begins . . .

First he assembles
a monitor screen
(a cardboard box
covered in tin foil
with a picture of the moon
scribbled on in orange crayon)

Next Space Boy clamps
on his plutonium space watch
(tin foil wrapped around his wrist)

Then Space Boy adjusts
his space visor (tin foil)

From here Space Boy prepares
a space suit for Cosmic Cat
(more tin foil)
which Cosmic Cat always refuses to wear

Next Space Boy tunes in
to the soundwaves of the cosmos
for news of alien sightings or invasions
(climbs under his duvet and twiddles the dial of his radio)

Then Space Boy inspects
the universe through his bio-force binary binoculars
(two toilet rolls with glued-on Cheerios AND tin foil)

Finally Space Boy ensures
that he is free from chronic-cosmic-contamination
(has a quick bath)

And some billion light years later
as Space Boy and Cosmic Cat
are whirling their way
through the intergalactic chaos of
encountering aliens
battling through black holes
and avoiding catastrophic galactic storms –
a horrible other-wordly screech
reaches their end of the universe
and stops them dead in their tracks:

'JAMES! Aren't you in bed yet?'

Dear Poet

We are class 4b
we read your book today you see
and thought that we would write to you
and ask you for your point of view
on many things. Is that OK?
We hope it is. Now anyway:

Do you always talk in rhyme?
Write your poems all the time?
Are you a really hunky guy?
Are all poets weird and shy?

Do you drive a fancy car?
Are you a famous megastar?
An A1 fab celebrity –
in the news and on TV?

Yours forever,

Class 4b

Dear 4b,

What can I say?
your letter really made my day!
and such great questions too, but oh –
to most of them the answer's 'No'!

No, I don't have a big flash car
and no great wealth. And megastar?!?
People say I've no great looks –
and famous? No – but do write books –

full of poems. I'm not shy –
or weird! But I'm a lucky guy:
with two great kids and lovely wife
wow, I have a super life:

writing poems all the time
(only sometimes talk in rhyme!)
Please write poems
send them too –

Yours,

A. Poet (Class 42!)

Take a Poem

Why not take a poem
wherever you go?
pop it in your pocket
nobody will know

Or take it to your classroom
stick it on the wall
tell your friends all about it
read it in the hall

Take it to the bathroom
tuck it up in bed
take the time to learn it
keep it in your head

Take it for a day trip
take it on a train
fold it as a hat
when it starts to rain

Take it to a river
fold it as a boat
pop it on the water
hope that it will float

Take it to a hilltop
fold it as a plane
throw it up skywards
time and time again

Take it to a postbox
send it anywhere
out into the world
with
            tender
                        loving
                            care

J.A.M.E.S. C.A.R.T.E.R.

James Winston Henry Carter (what are you sniggering at?) was born 27 November 1959. He can't remember a single thing about it.

Alice is James's strange but lovable cat. Or, more likely, James is Alice's strange but lovable owner. When they first met in the pet shop, Alice the month-old-kitten jumped on to James's shoulder. She still does this.

Mmmm . . . what else? James lives in Oxfordshire with his wonderful wife, Sarah, and two delightful daughters, Lauren and Madeleine, and not to forget the-cat-that-thinks-it's-a-parrot.

Every time he visits a school, children ask him, 'Where do you get your ideas from?' – to which he replies that he gets his ideas from the magic wood at the back of his house.

Seriously though, James believes there is a magic wood – your imagination – which takes things from your life, things that you've done, seen, read, daydreamed, remembered, and turns these into poems. Of the poems in this book, 'White Horse' is based on a dream he had about the white horse carved into the chalk hill at Uffington. 'Reindeer Haikus' was inspired by the reindeer skeleton in the Museum of Natural History in Oxford. Others, like 'Empty Bucket' and 'Fantasy Christmas List', are true stories.

Catching an idea when it comes, James believes, is essential. This is why he has an envelope in his pocket at all times – and because he heard that Paul McCartney wrote the lyrics to 'Hey Jude' on the back of an old envelope.

Always, always, always listening to music. James's particular faves include the Beatles, Tom Waits and XTC. To him, nothing beats playing 45s on his old record player! James feels that songs are like little poems wrapped up in music.

Reading (not Reading!) is something that he has always been mad about. As a boy he loved comics and Tintin books.

Trains are where he does most of his writing. James visits primary schools all over the UK, so catches a great many trains. If you ever see someone sat on a train writing a poem on an envelope, that could – just could – be him.

Electric guitars have been a lifelong passion. In fact, James takes his guitar (called Keith, of course) with him to play during his poetry performances. He likes doing this a) because it's great fun and b) it frightens the teachers a bit. He encourages children to bring along their air guitars and join in.

Reading (not reading!) is where James was born. He still can't remember anything about it. He wonders if Alice remembers that time in the pet shop . . .

A Poet a Week
Chosen by Paul Cookson

52 poets and 364 of the best poems of all time.
This contains a huge variety of forms and styles and all
manner of subject matter.

There are ballads, riddles, tongue-twisters, sonnets,
shape poems, raps, narrative verses and haikus; it
contains poems about seasons, festivals, animals, love,
war, life and death, food and football, to name a few.
There is also a biography of each poet at the beginning
of his or her week.

An essential book for teachers, but also a joyful
celebration of poets and poetry that readers will return
to again and again.

THE
WORKS 6

Every kind of poem you will ever
need for assembly, from poems about
faith, the environment, happiness and
friendship to poems about loss and
conflict. There are poems to celebrate
achievement and poems to help us deal
with the times we live in.

A book packed with gems for dipping
into time and time again.

A selected list of poetry titles available from
Macmillan Children's Books

The prices shown below are correct at the time of going to press.
However, Macmillan Publishers reserves the right to show new retail prices
on covers, which may differ from those previously advertised.

The Works 3: A Poet a Week   978-0-330-45181-9   £6.99

Chosen by Paul Cookson

The Works 6: Every kind of poem you will ever need for assembly

Chosen by Pie Corbett   978-0-330-43439-3   £6.99

Why Otters Don't Wear Socks

Poems by Roger Stevens   978-0-330-44851-2   £3.99

Behind the Staffroom Door

Poems by Brian Moses   978-0-230-01541-8   £3.99

All Pan Macmillan titles can be ordered from our website,
www.panmacmillan.com, or from your local bookshop
and are also available by post from:

Bookpost, PO Box 29, Douglas, Isle of Man IM99 1BQ
Credit cards accepted. For details:
Telephone: 01624 677237
Fax: 01624 670923
Email: bookshop@enterprise.net
www.bookpost.co.uk

Free postage and packing in the United Kingdom